GOSPEL GOLD

MORE SACRED TREASURES FOR PIANO

GlorySound

A DIVISION OF SHAWNEE PRESS, INC.
EXCLUSIVELY DISTRIBUTED BY HAL LEONARD CORPORATION

Visit Shawnee Press Online at
www.shawneepress.com

dedicated to Sue Call for her talents and many years of loyal service to
Cottage Grove Baptist Church, Cottage Grove, TN

BLESSED ASSURANCE, JESUS IS MINE

Tune: **ASSURANCE**
PHOEBE P. KNAPP (1839-1908)
Arranged by
MARY MCDONALD (ASCAP)

4

WHEN WE ALL GET TO HEAVEN

Tune: **HEAVEN**
EMILY D. WILSON (1865-1942)
Arranged by
BRAD NIX (ASCAP)

WHEN WE ALL GET TO HEAVEN

WHEN WE ALL GET TO HEAVEN

Count Your Blessings

Tune: **BLESSINGS**
EDWIN O. EXCELL (1851-1921)
Arranged by
PAMELA M. ROBERTSON

Laid back

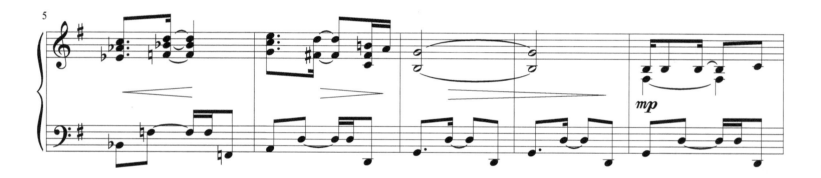

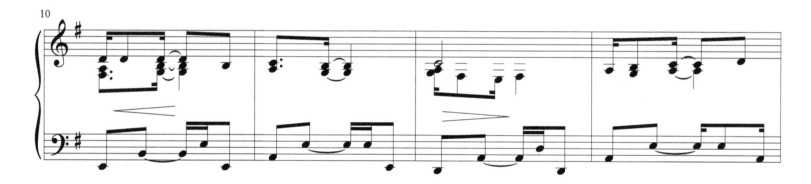

I Love to Tell the Story

Tune: **HANKEY**
WILLIAM G. FISCHER (1835-1912)
Arranged by JAMES KOERTS (BMI)

I LOVE TO TELL THE STORY

Revive Us Again

Tune: **REVIVE US AGAIN**
JOHN J. HUSBAND (1760-1825)
Arranged by
MARY MCDONALD (ASCAP)

for Todd King

Jesus Is All the World to Me

Tune: **ELIZABETH**
WILL L. THOMPSON (1847-1909)
Arranged by
VICKI TUCKER COURTNEY (ASCAP)

JESUS IS ALL THE WORLD TO ME

'Tis So Sweet to Trust in Jesus

Tune: **TRUST IN JESUS**
WILLIAM J. KIRKPATRICK (1838-1921)
Arranged by PAMELA M. ROBERTSON

'TIS SO SWEET TO TRUST IN JESUS

Tempo I

'TIS SO SWEET TO TRUST IN JESUS

TRUST AND OBEY

Tune: **TRUST AND OBEY**
DANIEL B. TOWNER (1850-1919)
Arranged by
PAMELA M. ROBERTSON

TRUST AND OBEY

TRUST AND OBEY

dedicated to Bobbie Brogdon, Volunteer Administrative Assistant,
Music Ministry, First Baptist Church, Easley, SC

THE OLD RUGGED CROSS

Tune: **OLD RUGGED CROSS**
GEORGE BENNARD (1873-1958)
Arranged by
CAROLYN HAMLIN (ASCAP)

With much sensitivity (♩=96)

THE OLD RUGGED CROSS

THE OLD RUGGED CROSS

THE OLD RUGGED CROSS

for Eric Case

At Calvary

Tune: **CALVARY**
DANIEL B. TOWNER (1850-1919)
Arranged by
JAMES KOERTS (BMI)

AT CALVARY

COME, YE THANKFUL PEOPLE, COME

Tune: **ST. GEORGE'S WINDSOR**
GEORGE J. ELVEY (1816-1893)
Arranged by
PAMELA M. ROBERTSON

Spirited (♩=144)

poco a poco rit.

Andante (with swing) (♩ = 100)

COME, YE THANKFUL PEOPLE, COME

COME, YE THANKFUL PEOPLE, COME

COME, YE THANKFUL PEOPLE, COME

Higher Ground

Tune: **HIGHER GROUND**
CHARLES H. GABRIEL (1856-1932)
Arranged by ALEX-ZSOLT (ASCAP)

HIGHER GROUND

dedicated to Connor Dalby

Ev'ry Time I Feel the Spirit

Traditional Spiritual
Arranged by
SHIRLEY BRENDLINGER

EV'RY TIME I FEEL THE SPIRIT

EV'RY TIME I FEEL THE SPIRIT

dedicated to Justin Knopp

Nobody Knows the Trouble I've Seen/
There Is a Balm in Gilead

Traditional Spirituals
Arranged by
SHIRLEY BRENDLINGER

NOBODY KNOWS THE TROUBLE I'VE SEEN/THERE IS A BALM IN GILEAD

NOBODY KNOWS THE TROUBLE I'VE SEEN/THERE IS A BALM IN GILEAD

NOBODY KNOWS THE TROUBLE I'VE SEEN/THERE IS A BALM IN GILEAD

ARE YOU WASHED IN THE BLOOD?

Tune: **WASHED IN THE BLOOD**
ELISHA A. HOFFMAN (1839-1929)
Arranged by
PAMELA M. ROBERTSON

(bring out melody)

ARE YOU WASHED IN THE BLOOD?

I'VE GOT PEACE LIKE A RIVER

Traditional Spiritual
Arranged by
ALEX-ZSOLT (ASCAP)

I'VE GOT PEACE LIKE A RIVER

I'VE GOT PEACE LIKE A RIVER

Contents
(Alphabetical Order)